Think Like A

Strategic Motherfucker

By:

Ryan Mason

Table of Contents

"Strategy without tactics is the slowest route to victory.

Tactics without strategy is the noise before defeat".

- Sun Tzu

Introduction

The ability to think strategically is one important skill you need to navigate life successfully. Why is this important? This is so important because most people's lives suck due to lack of strategic thinking, and it has been proven on the other hand that successful people are highly strategic thinkers. Every successful endeavour; from military, to business, to sports have all been achieved by intently applying the principles of strategic thinking. In the fields of military, business and professional sports, there's a long history of studying strategy. These fields are highly competitive and very demanding, they demand tangible concrete results. The individuals that come out victorious in military warfare, win in business, and win in sports are the best of the best because the stakes are very high in those fields.

We've got a pretty long history now, we've got a multi thousand year history of military campaigns that humanity has waged on itself that can be studied and picked apart, and we can find the lessons and distil the principles that work. We've also got a couple hundred years of real serious hard-core business that has been happening, we can study those principles and break them apart, and also we've got maybe a hundred years of professional sports that we can break down and break apart and find the juiciest principles, and what's amazing is that all of these apply to your personal life.

I want you to think of yourself as a general standing on the battlefield, and your task is not just to win the battle that's right in front of you, but to win the larger campaign; the war. Now the question is, what kind of a general are you? A successful general is a highly strategic general, he's the general that will win the battle and go on to win the war. The general that will fail and that will lose is the general who slacks off and doesn't understand the principles of proper strategy.

Most people do not engage in a methodical process of questioning, of evaluation, of assumptions, of investigation, of information gathering, analysis, planning, and finally taking action. Most people function in routines that they do not question, living life day to day, facing the same problems every day. People are always struggling with something, and their struggles haunt them till the day they die. People are always struggling with money, they are always quarrelling with their co-workers, or they're always dealing with inefficiencies in their work. The same exact inefficiencies, the same red tape, the same limitations, the same handicaps, the same relationship problems, they're always putting out some kind of fires or emergencies and it's always the same kind of fires, the same kind of emergencies. This is what the average person's life looks like, this is a person who's not strategic. Most people do not sit down and actually strategize, they don't strategize deeply enough and they don't strategize often enough, and in the end they make a lot of strategic blunders in their lives and they start wondering what's wrong with their lives? How come I hate my life?

'Think Like a Strategic Motherfucker' is a book that will help you achieve your goals both in business and personal life. Strategic thinking helps your business achieve its goals more rapidly. Success comes as a result of thinking about how you can proactively accomplish your objectives instead of just reacting to conditions. A strategic mind-set also encourages you to determine the best use of resources at your disposal and how to align them with your action plan.

Strategic Thinking Explained

So many meanings has been attributed to the term 'strategic thinking'. For instance, it has been defined as 'setting goals and developing flexible long-range plans to reach those goals based on careful analysis of internal and external environments'.

Strategic thinking is also 'thinking logically and deeply about the future. It means that where you want to be five years from now and five months from now and five days from now should inform what you do today'. Strategic thinking has also been defined as a way of 'looking at the world with a purpose in mind'. Furthermore, it has equally been defined as a way of dealing with a constantly changing environment by responding to that environment to achieve your goals and also attempting where possible, to change the environment to your benefit'. And lastly, Strategic Thinking is a method or a plan that we craft to bring about a desired future such as an achievement of a goal or a solution to a problem.

In sports, strategic thinking involves studying the competition, learning as much as you can about his tendencies, his habits and his weaknesses. Are you doing that? Who is the competition? Why do we even need to be strategic? Well, there is a competitor and the competitor is you. You are in battle with yourself, have you realized yet that you are your own greatest enemy? Have you realized yet that there's a battle inside of you going on every day? Between your lower self and your higher self? Between your ego and those spiritual drives, and those higher self-actualization drives within you that are pushing you towards becoming something much greater in your life? And that your lower self and your ego is extremely devious and extremely crafty and tricky and deceptive? It's the most deceptive thing that there is.

Strategic thinking involves studying ourselves, learning as much as we can about our own tendencies, our own habits, our own weaknesses our own self-deception mechanisms, the mechanisms by which we go unconscious, the way we sabotage ourselves the way we shoot ourselves in the foot, the way we go to war with ourselves. That's where we have to be extremely strategic. For most people, this is like a totally new concept. It doesn't even occur to them that this is something that they should be doing. I would say not only should you be doing this, this should be the prime focus of your life. The majority of your time in life needs to be going towards doing this, towards strategizing about your self-actualization that's what the majority of your life should be, that's what all your spare time should be spent thinking about.

It is very far for most people to get to this place, it'll take a lot of a lot of changing of your habits and your thought patterns to get to this point. I'm telling you get to see most people what they do is they commit major strategic blunders in their lives, the kind of blunders that would get you killed on a battlefield if you were this stupid and this short-sighted and this myopic and this slovenly.

Common Strategic Blunders & Mistakes

Many people do commit some strategic blunders at a very critical stage of their lives, this often have far-reaching consequences and most times prevent them from reaching their full potentials and living the lives of their dream. Let me give you a list of examples of some of the most common strategic blunders:

Getting married in your 20s, pissing away the prime years of your life; your teens and your twenties playing video games. Drinking and partying in college, not developing mastery of anything in life, eating junk food, chasing money rather than passion, chasing achievement and status rather than inner growth, having kids too soon in life, sticking it out with a bad boyfriend or a bad girlfriend that you know isn't right for you, not continuing your education after college or not even going to college or not even getting an education in the first place.

Another very big strategic blunder is staying loyal to a dysfunctional family member, investing money in the wrong places, thinking that you can get something for nothing in life, going into debt using credit cards, working 80 hours a week chasing success climbing the corporate ladder because you think it'll really get you somewhere, that's a huge strategic blunder, being too cheap to hire a therapist or life coach or being too cheap to buy books, or being too cheap to invest money in an online course, or an information product that could actually help you out. Being too cheap to go to a seminar or to a retreat that could help you out, living in the wrong place, hanging out with the wrong people, chasing sex or love, and devoting lots of your time and energy into it, neglecting meditation and taking your religion too seriously. These are huge strategic blunders. This is just a tip of the iceberg there are many more but these are the most common ones that easily comes to mind.

Let me talk about some of the strategic mistakes that people make, not these specific blunders but I want to talk about in general what are the failures of strategy that happened for people? Basically it's not doing the right things at the right time, it all boils down to that but I want to break that down into more specifics for you.

The first strategic mistake people make is not being able to think micro or macro. What does this mean? To be a good strategist in life, you need to be able to think macro which is the big picture, and then you need to be able to also think micro, which is the little logistical planning, the detail-oriented stuff. You need to be able to jump back and forth between micro and macro over and over again every single day. You need to be able to do this. Most people cannot do this, they don't know how to make the jump up or down, they get stuck either in the airy fairy dreamer land and they neglect the actual practical execution, or they get

14

lost in the minutiae of life, and they forget the ultimate goal of what they're trying to accomplish. Most people are terrible at this, and this is a skill that has to be developed, without this you cannot be strategic.

Another one is that people are not able to delay gratification. If you can't delay gratification, if you're always chasing just for pleasure or the most immediate gain, what strategy can you have? There cannot be a strategy if your strategy is immediate gain. Have you noticed that in all marketing efforts, everything that everyone ever sells you always plays on your weakness of delayed gratification? Everything promised to you is instant, it's fast, its flashy it's all the results that you'll get and then you get used to that and then what happens is that you just chase that stuff, and you forget that all the really important stuff in life comes through delayed gratification, it comes through strategy, no one just hands you valuable shit on a silver platter in life, you have to earn it through strategy and delayed gratification.

Could you imagine a general on the battlefield, and he's trying to win this big war, like world war 2 and you're the general who's been tasked with winning world war two for the Allies and your concern always in every meeting that you have with your staff and your military advisors and all your generals that are working under you is to always just go for the stuff that gives you immediate results, that would be a disastrous military campaign! Your forces would get defeated almost instantly.

Also people are generally bad strategists because they're unaware of the cul-de-sacs in life. The dead ends, the things they shouldn't do, the things that are traps, that are dangerous, that are costly, that are risky, they don't take these cul-de-sacs very seriously.

Also in general, people lack Intel. Could you imagine if I was a general on the battlefield, and I had to win this battle, but I had no intelligence whatsoever about the enemy, and I invested no time preparing the Intel, I didn't send out my spies, and I didn't bother to meet with them and get their reports to hear about what's actually going on the battlefield. I would just assume that I knew everything or just neglect the Intel altogether, that would be disastrous! And that's generally what people's lives are. There's zero Intel about self-actualization, zero Intel about meditation, zero Intel about enlightenment, zero Intel about life purpose and how to build a great career and how to start a business, zero intel on how to start a relationship, zero intel on what love is, and how love really works, zero intel on the mastery process, zero intel on the psychological development that happens throughout an adult's life.

What kind of results can you expect with zero Intel? How much energy are you devoting to building up your reserves of intelligence? For me, this is one of the most important things that I do in my life. My whole life is committed to developing my own intelligence, getting the information I need from multiple sources, not just one source because one source can be unreliable. Many sources, hundreds and thousands of hours devoted to gathering Intel because I need to be able to make important long-range strategic decisions and I can't do that without Intel.

Most people lack self-knowledge as well. How can you be strategic if you lack knowledge about yourself? If you don't know how you work? If you don't really study the machine that is the human mind, most people also neurotically overcompensate for the problems that they have in their lives, and this leads to a whole slew of strategic problems. Could you imagine a general who's always reacting to problems on the battlefield, he's not proactive, he's not planning his own strategy but he's just always reactive. Neurotically reacts if he gets pissed off and angry and he gets jealous and sad, and he's just always overreacting, that would be a terrible general. Yeah, this is how most people live their lives, and then, they're surprised at the results they see.

Another huge strategic mistake people make is chasing the small prize rather than the large prize. They don't know how to evaluate outcomes and they don't know how to prioritize to really judge. Okay , this is nice, but then that's a bigger prize, so that thing is worth more than this thing, and then there's a third thing that's even a bigger prize than this thing and maybe there's this other factor that renders both of these things or this third thing not even as valuable as I thought it was. So sometimes we have a deception, we think something is a big prize, but then we realize it's not a big prize, it's actually a small prize.

What's the biggest prize? What should I be going after? Should I be fighting this battle here or that battle there? Or maybe I shouldn't engage in any of these battles for now, and I'll pick a new battle in six months to fight the one that's really going to matter. Most people don't go through this process, they just kind of do the thing that lands on their lap without really questioning from up, from a ground zero position. They don't really question is this even necessary? Why am I doing this? In the big picture what's it going to mean? People can be very hard workers they can spend 80 hours of a week working on something for 20 years, but the thing they're working on is a small prize.

Another strategic mistake that people commit is that they are generally oblivious to social and business traps. Do you know, and have you studied the traps that culture society and business has laid for you? These traps are like minefields. These traps exist in religion, in education, in the culture at large, in politics, in your social circle, in the advertising media.

All these traps are designed to trick you and to catch you, to take your money, to get you involved with the wrong thing that doesn't serve you but serve somebody else. You must understand that generally speaking, the aims of businesses and social organizations is not to really help you, the aims of most of these organizations is to serve themselves at your expense. Their aim is to feed off of you, to leech off you. But most people don't understand this. Most people just play into it, and they think they're actually getting benefited by this leeching. In contrast, these businesses and social organizations are parasitic, they suck your life energy away from you and rob you of any ability that you have of really self-actualizing and growing to your full potential and contributing meaningfully to life and improving society.

A really good general goes out onto the battlefield on the morning before the battle and analyses the landscape. He looks and sees areas the enemy could have laid a trap for his army. You know that hill over there, that's a suspicious-looking hill. there's some trees there and there's a little patch of grass, there could be some enemies lurking there, hidden lying in wait for me tomorrow when we start this campaign or what about that river down there, maybe there's a some kind of dangerous trap in that river that I need to think about, be careful of, so that when I'm crossing that river, my troops don't get slaughtered. Most people don't do this with their personal lives.

Also another trap people fall into is that they don't invest time strategizing. The average time that a person invests per week strategizing about life is zero. Could you imagine a general who spent zero time strategizing about his military campaigns, he just rushed head-on into every campaign and just kind of flew by the seat of his pants, that general would be dead very soon. See, in terms of military, the reason I like military strategy is because the stakes are so high, you're talking about people's lives, and you're talking about your own life. In modern times when a general loses a battle he doesn't even lose his head, but a thousand years ago or 2,000 years ago if you study Roman military strategy for example, or ancient Chinese military strategy, stuff like Sun Tzu, the general was the first one to lose his head. It was always his head that was on the line, so he took his strategy extremely seriously in a way that even modern generals can't really appreciate because their lives are not on the line. The president's life is not on the line when he chooses to invade a country, this was not the case 2,000 years ago; his life was on the line so he was much smarter about this.

It's good that you know this because it really makes you sober, very sober and much invested in making the right choices and the right strategies. Nowadays, it is so easy to be complacent in life, you know, we live in a pretty comfortable society, you can scrape- by pretty easily without being very strategic, so people get lazy, the stakes aren't high in their minds and so because of this, they don't strategize and they piss their life away by default.

Another huge strategic mistake people make is not fixing problems at their root. Most people only care about fixing problems on the surface, not at the root. The commitment to fix a problem at the root is a very rare thing, I see it so rarely. To me, it is a character trait, you either have this character trait or you don't, and most people don't. They just don't care about fixing problems at their root, they just want to fix something enough that they can just go on with their life, keep coasting. That's not how I think, that's terrible because what this means is that in the future, that problem will come back to bite you in the ass, and I don't know about you, but if I face a problem, I want to solve it permanently so it never ever comes back to bite me in the ass.

And lastly, most people don't spend any time developing their strategic resources I'll talk more about this as we go on because this is one of the pillars that I'm going to share with you is strategic preparation.

You got to prepare your resources. What are the resources that you will need in life to live the kind of life that you want to live? I don't know about you, but personally, my life as early on as I can remember has always been about strategizing, about what resources should I build for myself, whether it's more money that I need or I need a certain amount of time, I need to be in a certain place, I need to live in a certain city, I need to live in a different part of the country, I need to have a certain kind of education or a certain piece of knowledge or a certain skill set, I need to go and build and develop those resources.

Can you imagine a general on a battlefield who rushes into battle with no strategic resources? He hasn't prepared food for the troops, he hasn't arranged logistical support, air support, and none of these things have been thought of or taken care of, he has zero resources. Besides, he's going in to the battle with all he's got he's got, no reserves, he's got no backup plans, he's got nothing. He's going to get slaughtered, and that's what happens to most people in life.

So let me tell you now in a nutshell the seven pillars of strategic thinking. And I'll cover each one in some depth and tell you about it. So you need to have strategic intent for there to be a strategy at all, I'll talk about that in a minute the second pillar is strategic analysis and gathering of intelligence, pretty self-explanatory but I'll cover it as well. Also the third one is strategic preparation, that's what I was just talking about, preparing your resources for battle. The fourth principle is concentration of force. Fifth pillar is disciplined execution and detailed tactical follow-through the sixth pillar is adaptability and the seventh pillar is the study of general principles so let's talk about each one of these pillars and some details

PILLAR ONE
Strategic Intent

At the center of any truly great strategy, we find a pure crystalline core. Business schools call this strategic intent, but it can go by other names; vision, direction, big idea, dream, Holy Grail, El Dorado etc. Without this vibrant core, you have no strategy, you have only aimless technique, perhaps a catchy slogan like "when the going gets tough the tough get going". Now strategic intent animates any great adventure, whether accompanied by practical strategy or not. I take the legend of King Arthur and his knights of the round table, a quasi-myth that began in the 5th or 6th century. Arthurian legend offers us a fabulous example of the hero's quest. The hero's quest is a universal story, and it's the framework for virtually every inspirational and successful utterance of strategic intent. Every great strategy begins with a big idea. Strategic intent is the articulation of a powerful achievable and motivating stretch goal. No strategy can succeed without it, in fact, no plan can be considered a legitimate strategy without a powerful vision or an intent.

Historical figures as disparate as King Arthur, Napoleon, Vince Lombardi, Bismarck Woodrow Wilson, and Martin Luther King all have articulated powerful strategic visions. Strategic intent at the core of any plan is a great idea, any action plan without strategic intent is best likened to an engine without fuel, which is the unfortunate reality of many so-called strategies, slogans, procedures, techniques, or tactics to give an appearance of strategy great sound and fury but nothing at the core.

Let's begin with a clear notion of what constitutes strategic intent. Two influential scholars coined the term and relate their concept of strategic intent in the Harvard Business Review. Gary Hamel and CK Prahlada have been two of the most influential business thinkers of the last 50 years, and together they created the concept of core competency in business analysis. In fact, the Wall

Street Journal called Gary Hamel the world's most influential business thinker, and Fortune magazine called him the world's leading expert on business strategy. Now as with many modern ideas, this idea of strategic intent has been around for a long time, much longer without a name than with. In fact, the timeless Universal story of the hero's quest captures the essence of the idea.

Prahlada and Hamel gave new form in their treatment of strategic intent. These two thinkers recognize the great flaw in much of our thinking about strategy. Up until the 1990s, this flaw was the pursuit of imitative techniques as a substitute for strategy, they called it a strategy of imitation. Now instead, strategic intent inspires a company or a person or an army or a team with an obsession of winning at every level of the organization. But it's not simply ambition, strategic intent articulates the long term vision or aspiration of the company, it means reaching for something beyond your current capabilities and developing resources to accomplish that goal. Current capabilities and resources are just not sufficient, and so this forces you to become more inventive and resourceful. In a world where resources are scarce, this is called establishing stretch goals.

An older more traditional view is to tailor your ambition to current capabilities, but this is in reality a formula for just maintaining the status quo. Now on the other hand, stretch goals without strategic intent are a recipe for failure.

The concept of stretch goals linked to strategic intent is one of the secrets to the Japanese economic renaissance in the aftermath of World War 2. It entails envisioning a future that seems near impossible, and then striving to acquire the capabilities and resources to make that future possible. Numerous Japanese companies adopted versions of this philosophy. Honda, Mitsubishi, Sony, and Toyota to mention a few.

Now, strategic intent means identifying an extreme gap between resources and our ambitions, and then developing a strategy to fulfil those ambitions. Let's look at a variety of examples of strategic intent.

Expert mythologist, Joseph Campbell identified the hero's journey as the archetypal story that is animated in all societies. Throughout history, every man and every woman knows this story and is moved by it. The hero's quest is the story of Prometheus stealing fire of Ulysses, quest for home after the Trojan War, Jason and the Golden Fleece, King Arthur's Knights of the Round Table, and the quest for the Holy Grail of the real world stories of modern movie heroes Luke Skywalker. In this adventures, the hero finds the strength within himself to conquer all obstacles, no matter how impossible. It is transformation through triumphs with establishing of your own strategic intent it's useful to keep in mind the story of the hero's quest.

Now this sounds grandiose and far from your world, it's not. Your life is filled with heroes and villains, conflict and conquest, failure and triumph, your story is what you contrived and the ease of it is that your story elements are all decided for you, its characters, its impersonal forces, its plot, the villain, the conflict, the climax, and the identity of the hero you need to become.

The hero's quest is an epic, when thought-out and articulated, it can provide high tone power and purpose, the hero's quest provides you with the framework, the hero's quest ends with the ship in homeport, the Knight saving his princess, the union preserved, social justice achieved, the journey brought to successful conclusion. Now perhaps, its biggest advantage is that it resonates with people, the story sounds familiar, it sounds comfortable.

Now, if we move from mythology, one of the clearest examples of strategic intent comes from the world of sports. Few men embodied the idea of strategic intent as much as the late great football coach, Vince Lombardi. Lombardi was the legendary coach of the NFL's Green Bay Packers, and he won the first two Super Bowls in the mid-1960s, his grasp of strategic intent was sure and unambiguous. He used it well "winning isn't everything it's the only thing". This quote may have originated elsewhere, but it has forever been linked to Lombardi. Its corollary is equally powerful and unambiguous, "show me a good loser and I'll show you a loser". No compared to the endlessly qualified rhetoric and ambiguity that permeates modern society, these phrases crash on us as powerful and unsettling. It's their clarity they'll act compromised they leave no wiggle, no room for waffling, they leave no escape for excuse, they are unequivocal.

Every strategy requires a powerful strategic intent to animate it, equally, our intent must also be translated into achievable mid-range goals, whether it's our personal strategy or a strategy for an entire organization. Now to take our Vince Lombardi example, the famous coach did not stop at articulating a powerful intent that could easily stand alone as a catchphrase or a motivational slogan, he did not say the game comes down to who wants it more, no, he made the intent tangible for his players here is how;

Lombardi translated the overall goal of winning into a clear statement of strategic intent, making it crystal clear for each of his players, he said this: "you never win a game unless you beat the guy in front of you".

To score on the board doesn't mean a thing, that's for the fans. You've got to win the war with the man in front of you, you've got to get your man. Now if we consider a football team as a value chain, with victory dependent on each player's individual effort and continuous high performance, It is clear how this notion of strategic intent fits into strategic planning. It's also clear that mere technique can never successfully substitute for strategic intent. At every level in an organization or private life, strategic intent backed up by a clearly articulated plan and tactics is key to every winning battle.

Now, two more very famous examples come from two very contrasting arenas, the first is competition between nations, and the second is competition between good and evil. Both are sterling examples of the power of strategic intent, coupled with the appropriate tactics. Both examples come from the 1960s, and they were articulated by two of the most influential leaders in American history.

The first comes from John F Kennedy. President Kennedy was faced with a Soviet threat that appeared as a powerful and plausible alternative to the democracies of the West. Soviet technology had beaten the U.S. into space with the first satellite in 1957, and it put the first man into orbit in early 1961. An America's own early effort was feeble by comparison, a 15-minute suborbital flight in May of that year.

Now, confronted with this challenge, Kennedy gauged the mood of the nation and he responded with boldness, he didn't call for imitation of the Soviets, he didn't call for continuous process improvement. Instead, Kennedy issued a brilliant articulation of strategic intent, his statement of intent was clear, concise, and bold and it fired the imagination of the nation. "we choose to go to the moon in this decade and do the other things not because they are easy, but because they are hard, because that goal will serve to organize and measure the best of our energies and skills, because that challenge is one that we will to accept one we are unwilling to postpone and one we intend to win". NASA responded brilliantly with the Saturn 5, booster in project Apollo, and a host of new technological advances throughout the 1960s that achieved Kennedy's goal, less than 10 years later, on July 20th 1969, when astronaut, Neil Armstrong set foot on the moon.

Kennedy already had a strategy for achieving his strategic vision even before he made the speech, he had already asked his adviser how can we beat the Russians in space, and scientist Werner von Braun had already sent a memo, arguing that the Soviets would be difficult to beat in the short term, but that the wealthy US could leap ahead to invest in rocket technology. The Soviet Union didn't yet know how Kennedy's strategic intent was granted but it was grounded in a realistic strategy.

Strategic intent can animate nations to great technological achievements as we may see again in the space race between China and India. It can also animate people to overturn social injustice even against overwhelming odds. Martin Luther King exemplifies the melding of a powerful strategic intent and vision. With a perfectly executed strategy, he marshalled the forces of an entire nation with a vision of social justice embodied in his dream, and he crafted a strategy whereby every single person could execute this strategy as a significant player, the strategy of non-violent civil disobedience.

Now let's consider another example from international politics. For 40 years after the end of World War 2, the United States engaged in a worldwide competition with its main rival; the Soviet Union. This was called the Cold War, and it began in the period after World War 2. It was an ideological struggle between democracy and communism. In the words of Winston Churchill, "an Iron Curtain had descended between East and

West". the United States pursued a single coherent foreign policy for all of those years, inspired by a core strategic intent, that policy had as its touchstone, a strategic intent inspired by American diplomat George Kennan, in the immediate post-war world war 2 world, the Soviet Union emerged as a threat to the democracies of Western Europe, and to the stability of the entire system of States. The Western response was erratic, reactive and incoherent, it wasn't clear what Soviet intent was, or how to respond in a way that could avert nuclear disaster.

This situation continued until 1946 when diplomat George Kennan sent his famous classified telegram from the US Embassy inside the Soviet Union and it was later published in foreign affairs magazine in July of 1947, the telegram was published in foreign affairs as the sources of Soviet conduct. The logic behind the analysis was that the Soviet leadership was impervious to reason, but was highly sensitive to the logic of force. The reasonable extension of this assumption was that the US ought to meet Soviet power with American power, where actual power was not used, the Soviets should face America.

America resolve the proper response then of the United States was to contain Soviet expansionist schemes by meeting the Soviet challenge where ever arose worldwide. At the core of this was a strategic intent of containment, and this became the foundation of American foreign policy for the next 40 years. Containment served as a succinct and clear articulation of US strategic intent, there was no sloganeering to be number one in the field. In fact, the United States was a reluctant leader but the U.S. eventually triumphed as first, Eastern Europe was liberated from communist oppression in 1989, followed by the collapse of the Soviet Union in 1991.

From the earliest 21st century, we have a superb textbook example of the power of strategic intent from India's largest multinational conglomerate under the leadership of a visionary Indian businessman, Ratan Tata. Ratan Tata is the chairman of the Tata Group, and he established a clear strategic intent for his automotive company.

In 2003, he envisioned a four passenger vehicle, meeting minimum safety and emission standards that the average Indian could afford, but it was to be much more than simply another cheap automobile. Tata articulated a strategic intent that no other person in his company believed possible at the time. He insisted that it was to be the world's cheapest automobile, the people's car and it would cost no more than one lakh, at the time two thousand dollars. His engineers balked at this, but Tata would not budge and he insisted on the price and a brutal timetable, they met both.

The result was the unveiling of the Tata Nano in early 2008, a tiny inexpensive four passenger automobile designed and built in India, and the end product of an incredible focus and vision of one man, Ratan Tata. Tata said that: Today, we indeed have a people's car which is affordable and yet built to meet safety requirements, fuel efficient and low on emissions. But the Nano did much more than provide inexpensive transportation for the poorest Indians, its innovative cost-cutting measures have revolutionized the way automobiles are made and sold in price in size and distribution and in technology.

Now, we've looked at powerful and successful examples of strategic intent. When strategic intent is absent however, a company can lose its focus, and it can drift and ends up in crisis. A company with no strategic intent can collapse. Let's turn to what happens when in business when a company refuses to state its strategic intent.

Digital Equipment Corporation is an example of a company that refused to make the hard choices necessary for coherent strategy, and it found itself paralyzed, unable to even articulate a coherent strategic intent. In 1992, the company was faced with the necessity of charting its strategic direction, in what was a chaotic electronics industry. The company could not decide on one of three directions advocated by passionate adherents within the senior leadership. Whether to manufacture chips, or to offer customers consulting solutions, or finally to build computers. So the company compromised, the company issued this statement: Digital Equipment Corporation is committed to providing high quality products and services and being a leader in data processing".

Now this statement is a pretence, it's like whitewash on a rotting fence, its vague language and its lack of focus as an indicator of faltering leadership, it was surely not designed to rally the troops at a time of company crisis, six years after this debacle the company was swallowed by Compaq.

Now, let me issue a caveat here, to note that a powerful focused strategic intent is not sufficient for securing the ends of your strategic plan, misguided intent can be just as bad as no intent at all. Here is an example from the business world.

The proud company Levi-Strauss, makers of possibly the most famous blue jeans in history, under CEO Bob Hass who assumed command from 1984 to 1999. Levi's adopted a strategic vision that was nothing short of bizarre, according to some observers. Competitive intelligence expert, Bin Jawad, contends that Levi's was a classic case of a leader with a vision, but the vision did not match reality. Levi's market share then plummeted from 1990 to 2000, from 48 percent of the market down to 17 percent.

Another example on a far greater scale than a single company comes from Imperial Japan in the 1930s, the grandiose Japanese strategic intent of the late 1930s offers a good lesson in strategic intent gone awry. Japan wanted to rectify many of the perceived injustices of the colonial period in Asia, Southeast Asia and the Pacific. Imperial Japan envisioned an Asian region free of the Western powers, but under its own leadership, and this region was to be called the Greater East Asia co-prosperity sphere. This forced would-be economic alliance was purported to be a new international order that sought a euphemistic co-prosperity for countries throughout Asia. This of course was really a front for Japanese imperialist ambitions and it led to the establishment of puppet regimes in every place the Japanese were ascendant but every student of history knows now that Japan overreached, it did not have the capabilities to match its ambitions and while its strategy worked for a time, in the long run it was not tenable.

And as a final example of a powerful and successful statement of strategic intent. Consider this powerful statement by one of America's most revered leaders, Abraham Lincoln. President Lincoln grappled with the greatest trial of any president in American history, he faced the real possibility of the dissolution of the country by bloody civil war, he was forced to wage war against his countrymen, but he did not wage war simply and reactively and as a mere technical process, no, he waged war with strategic intent of maintaining the Union as a country free for all men, breathing life into those ideals put to paper almost a century earlier. These were ideals he's so eloquently framed already two years before he became president. During his first speech as a candidate for the US Senate in 1858, "a house divided against itself cannot stand, I believe this government cannot endure permanently half slave and half free. I do not expect the Union to be dissolved, I do not expect the house to fall but I do expect it will cease to be divided it will become all one thing or all the other".

And then, in one of the most powerful expressions of strategic intent ever articulated the Gettysburg Address delivered as a eulogy for those who died in battle begins with these famous words "four score and seven years ago, our fathers brought forth on this continent a new nation. conceived in Liberty and dedicated to the proposition that all men are created equal" and the Gettysburg Address concludes with a ringing statement of strategic intent "we here highly resolve that these dead shall not have died in vain, that this nation under God shall have a new birth of freedom and that government of the people by the people for the people shall not perish from the earth from foreign policy to social policy to business to sports to myth and even legend to the preservation of the Union."

Strategic intent provides a powerful impetus to drive cogent strategy and to motivate people to implement that strategy. Without strategic vision is just soulless technique. It's a great flurry of activity akin to that of a treadmill. We see this too often as part of the strategic masquerade, there is nothing Courageous about making a bold pronouncement in vague language. Sloganeering in the language of market leadership or hat tipping to shareholder wealth or to the pursuit of excellence lack of strategic intent this means a loss of focus and the routinization of process.

Continuous improvement is neither strategic intent nor strategy. Being the best I can be is neither a strategic intent nor is it a strategy. We've seen that articulating a strategic intent requires boldness, grounded in a strategic and accurate assessment of reality, it means charting a course and closing off some options because you have elected consciously to pursue one goal with single-minded fervour. With regard to strategic intent and our own lives, too often we perhaps think too modestly, we look only at our resources and we trim our ambitions accordingly.

Look we can't all be Abraham Lincoln or Martin Luther King Jr. but we can and we should set seemingly impossible goals, acquire the necessary resources and develop a strategy to attain those goals

Finally remember that strategic intent is a compelling vision of the future that motivates action. This is what elevates a technique into a strategy. It is the ultimate thing that you're going for. What's the ultimate outcome you want? The ultimate outcome needs to inform all the steps that lead up to it, all the actions you take when you're highly strategic you're highly efficient about this, you don't just take random actions; you don't just go and fight random battles just for the sake of fighting battles. Think about this, if a nation is fighting a war against another nation, this is an extremely costly endeavour, it has to be motivated by some sort of ultimate strategic intent. What's the point? What do you want? Usually you want something and you better be specific about it. You can't be vague and wishy-washy, you're not just there to fight; you're there to accomplish a goal. Do you want to annex the enemy's territory? Do you want to fight to ensure peace? Do you want to change laws? Do you want to conquer the people? Do you want to enslave them? What do you want? You have to be very clear about that, until you're clear about that you can't have any strategy whatsoever this is called strategic intent.

Once you have your strategic heading, you're very clear about it. Now what you can do is you can backwards engineer every step necessary to achieve your goals. For instance, if you're going to do a very long road trip that's a thousand miles long, you better know where you want to end up. Because if you just start driving in any random direction, you're basically never going to be satisfied with the way your trip will end, because you're not going to know which way to turn. Every turn in the way will be sufficiently good. You can't make decisions based on that.

Most people have zero strategic content in their personal lives, they have no big picture, they have no overarching vision, nothing that compels them towards action or towards planning of any kind, which is why no planning or action really happens, and they complain about lack of motivation and lack of results. What people do is they just apply techniques and take random steps, thinking that this is strategy, when in fact, it's not just applying the techniques in your life, may be a little bit here, a little bit there, that's not enough to get to the kind of life that we're talking about. You need to be much of a big-picture thinker than that. You got to see 10, 20. 30 years down the road of what you're shooting for, and then everything that you do today and tomorrow, and the next week, in the next month, and next year has to all be methodically aligned with that. Every single day, you have to wake up and ask yourself, is this action that I'm taking aligning me and moving me closer to my ultimate strategic intent, or is it not? Most of the actions you're taking in your life, in fact right now are irrelevant and tangential or even worse, they're slowing you down and distracting you from achieving your strategic intent.

It's very easy for the mind to trick itself into thinking that, oh just because I'm taking this action here, or I'm doing this process here, that this is getting me to where I want to go, that's rarely the case, very rarely the case. It's very rare to meet a human being who has a very clear and strong strategic intent, and if you do meet such a person, you'll see that this person accomplishes amazing things in their life that seem impossible to the other people. This is why the general needs to know whether the battle he's going to fight here tomorrow is actually going to advance him towards his ultimate purpose of winning the war. Just because you win a battle does not mean that it gets you closer to winning the war. This is something that has to be always checked and asked and verified over and over again, will winning this battle actually get me closer to winning the war? No? Then, let's not fight this battle let's save our reserves and use them where it really is going to count that's how you have to think.

PILLAR TWO

Strategic analysis and gathering of intelligence

The second pillar is strategic analysis. This is the analysis of the strengths and weaknesses and opportunities and threats that present themselves on the battlefield. Are you assessing, acquiring and allocating the necessary resources in the most effective and efficient uses possible? How do you allocate your time and your energy and your physical vitality and your charisma and your attention span? How are you allocating all these things? What are you putting these things towards in your life? Are you using these things efficiently and effectively to move you towards your ultimate strategic intent?

Also as part of strategic analysis you have to anticipate and incorporate competitor responses because the battlefield is not a static place, it's a very flexible and fluid situation, it is always changing, your competitors are smart, they're also scheming and strategizing against you. So you have to strategize and anticipate that and incorporate their potential responses in your strategy.

Now what am I talking about, who's the competition again? The competition is not your business competitors, the competition is not your family members or your friends; the competition is yourself.

When we're talking about self-actualization are you anticipating the responses of your ego and your lower self when you're trying to grow, when you're trying to make a change in your life, are you anticipating how your subconscious mind is going to react? How it's going to resist? How it's going to rebel? How it's going to trick you, the excuses it will tell you, how it will trap you, how it will convince you that you shouldn't change. Most people have no awareness of this whatsoever and so of course the competition always wins, the lower self always wins.

SWOT analysis is an effective process that typically businesses and companies use to analyse themselves and their competitors and formulate their strategies. SWOT is nothing but an acronym for strengths and weaknesses, and opportunities and threats. This important exercise can be very helpful for us individuals, whether you're looking for a new job, or trying to climb the corporate ladder or working on your life goals. A personal SWOT analysis can help you achieve your goals.

It is a creative method of self-assessment to help you assess where your life or career is, and where it could go. To conduct a personal SWOT analysis, ask yourself questions about each of the four areas being examined and answer honestly. Honesty is crucial or the analysis will not generate meaningful results. With that in mind, try to see yourself from the standpoint of a colleague, or a bystander, and view criticism with objectivity. Don't limit yourself to the strengths that you're currently exhibiting in your life, or in your job, list all of your strengths even the ones that have been dormant for a while and pay particular attention to the things that you have that your peers don't. How are you different unique and special?

The next step is weaknesses. This part examines the areas in which you need to improve and the things that will set you back in your life and your career.

For the opportunities, look at the external factors that you can take advantage of to pursue your goals and dreams be it at work or be it in your life.

Finally, look at any threats to your career or life growth. This part takes into account the external factors that could hurt your chances to attain your goals. Once you have filled out the matrix, there are two ways to analyse the information and build a strategy matching or converting matching means connecting two of the categories to determine a course of action for example matching strengths to opportunities shows you where to action. On the other hand, matching weaknesses to threats exposes those areas you should work on, or situations to avoid, and lets you know where to be more defensive of your position. To convert is to turn negatives into positives. In other words, converting your weaknesses into strengths or threads into opportunities this can mean growing a skill set through education or maybe finding a creative way to feature a weakness as a strength.

Once the personal SWOT analysis is completed, it is crucial to follow through on the insights you uncovered. SWOT analysis can fail to be effective if it's simply treated as a laundry list without any time to how the elements identified in the analysis can be put into play. For example, how can the identified strengths move the needle in the end ever to achieve a key goal? Or how can one navigate a potential threat once it is identified so as to ensure no ground is lost? The best outcome is to take action and succeed in the opportunities you have identified. This can benefit you on a personal and a professional level and set you apart from your peers and colleagues.

PILLAR THREE

Strategic Preparation

I have already touched on this but let me go into some more depth. What this means is the building up of strategic reserves through preparation. Your manoeuvres will be limited if you have no reserves. Therefore, you must prepare. So again, a general on a battlefield, he wants to make sure that his troops have flexibility, he needs to provide them with weapons with armour, with vehicles, with support, with food, with water, with clothing, with shelter, with the back-up plan, with a retreat location they can go back to, with some kind of support structure so that they don't get bombarded from the air or by arrows.

He's to think about all these stuffs he then use them to prepare and lay the groundwork. It's not just about rushing in there and coming up with the best tactical move on the battlefield that wins the war, no, a lot of times, wars are won or lost based on how well you prepare for the war. Do you have enough food for the winter? Do you have enough water? If you neglect these very basics, then you will get slaughtered on the battlefield. And most people in life neglect these basics.

What does it really mean to do strategic preparation? It means thorough training, it means hard work, it means discipline, it means sound planning and then, it also means the preparation of your unique capabilities. Every soldier on the battlefield or every unit of soldiers on the battlefield has unique capabilities, it has unique strengths and also unique weaknesses and limitations. Cavalry has certain strengths that infantry doesn't have and vice versa, and then your spearmen have different capabilities than your archers, and your archers have different capabilities than your aerial units or whatever.

You need to recognize what these unique abilities are, and the need to develop these in yourself. What are your unique abilities in your personal life? Are you developing those? How much time are you spending preparing and bolstering your unique capabilities in life? How many hours a week are you spending doing that? For most people, it's zero. And of course, we wonder why we get crap results. Here's a quote that's relevant to strategic preparation "since you can't predict what fortune will hand you, you must develop yourself internally to handle the external circumstances".

You must develop yourself internally to handle the external circumstances. What else is this describing but self-actualization? This is what self-actualization is about, developing yourself internally to handle the external circumstances of life.

Most people spend no attention to this at all, they pay no mind to it whatsoever and then they fail miserably. Personally in my own, life I spend the majority of my life in strategic preparation mode I'm highly strategic when it comes to preparation because I know that this is one of the variables that I can control the best. I can't always predict what's going to happen on the battlefield, and I'm not always the quickest on the battlefield, but I can really sit down and prepare my resources in extremely strategic way, that gives me so much leverage and so much manoeuvrability on the battlefield that it's very hard for me to lose the Battle.

Action Plan for Achieving Your Goals

Everyone has goals, but some seem to accomplish far more than others. That's because people who accomplish goals at a higher rate than the average person are those who use a systematic proven method of goal-setting and goal attainment. The answer is simple, you need an effective action plan.

The first step in creating an action plan is deciding exactly what you want. Clarity is the most important single quality of goal setting, and perhaps, the most important single quality of success. Instead of fuzzy goals like; more money, better health and happiness. Be specific about exactly how much money you want to earn in a specific period of time, or what level of health and fitness or weight that you desire. You need to set goals that are multi-dimensional, and for every part of your life so that you function like a well-oiled goal setting goal achieving machine. You need goals for your health, your career, your finances, your relationships, your personal and professional development, and your community and spiritual growth. This will immediately put you in a separate category from people, because most people have no idea what they really want. Most people are unconsciously preoccupied with the fear of failure, which blocks them from setting clear specific goals. If you don't set clear specific goals, then, you can't fail to achieve them because they're so vague, this is a major reason for failure.

Next, weight your goals or goal down on a sheet of paper, only 3% of adults have written goals, and everyone else plans to write them down someday. Success begins with a piece of paper, a pen, and a few minutes of time. You can start with the three goal method in less than 30 seconds, quickly write down your three most important goals in life right now, whatever three goals you manage to write down is probably an accurate picture of what you really want in life. When you actually write a goal down, it is as if you are programming it into your subconscious mind and activating a whole series of mental powers that will enable you to accomplish much more than you ever dreamed of, you begin to expect to achieve the goal and you start to attract people and circumstances into your life that are consistent with the attainment of your goal.

The third step is setting a deadline. If it's a large goal, set a series of sub deadlines. And what if you don't achieve your goal by the deadline? Set another deadline! Remember a deadline is just a guesstimate of when you will achieve it, you may achieve the goal well in advance, or it may take you much longer than you expect, but you must have a target time before you. Setting off a deadline acts as a forcing system on your subconscious mind toward achieving your goal on schedule, as you want to achieve financial independence you may set a 10 or 20 year goal, and then break it down year by year, so that you know how much you have to save and invest each year. There are no unreasonable goals, only unreasonable deadlines.

The next step in creating an action plan is making a list of everything that you could possibly think of that you will have to do to achieve your goal. After having a written goal, one of the things that holds people back is not taking the time to lay out the list of all the little things they will have to do to get there. Identify the obstacles that you will have to overcome, identify the knowledge, information, and skills you will need, and then, identify the people whose help and cooperation you will require to achieve your goal.

The more comprehensive your list, the more motivated you will be, the more intense will be your desire, and the more you will believe it is possible. Combine all these things into a plan, organized by priority and sequence priorities was more important and less important sequence is what you have to do before you do something else and in what order. List every single step that you can think of that you have to follow. as you think of new items add them to your list the 80/20 rule says that 80% of your results will come from 20% of your activities the 20/80 rule says that the first 20% of time that you spend planning your goal organize your plan will be worth 80 percent of the time and effort required to achieve the goal. Now that you have this comprehensive list, schedule into a comprehensive plan. Plan each day, week, and month in advance, plan each month at the beginning of the month, plan each week the weekend before, and plan each day the evening before. The more careful and details you are when you plan your activities and tasks.

As you go through each day of your plan select your number one most important goal for the day, again, you can set your priorities with the 80/20 rule. Ask yourself, if I can only do one thing on this list, which one activity is most important? Then ask yourself, if I could only do one other task on this list, which one would be the most valuable use of my time? Then write a number 2 next to it, now keep asking this question until you have the top 20% of your tasks organized by sequence and priority, and now you have an action plan. Your next step is to take action, keep track of your progress and make adjustments along the way. Make sure you're doing something every day to move you in the direction of what you really want in life.

PILLAR FOUR

Concentration of Force

"Concentration of force at the decisive point is the key to all strategy it's all about directing as much force to one point as possible given your limited resources this applies to war as much as it applies to career development and to business".

The next pillar is concentration of force. This is a super important concept which is studied and taught in all military schools and in any classes where you're studying military battles and tactics. Because to win a military battle, it's fundamentally what has to happen be; you have to concentrate force at a point, at a decisive point that breaks through into victory. Are you even aware that this is what strategy is all about? It's all about finding the weak point on the battlefield and then pushing all your troops at that weak point to get a breakthrough, and that's a battlefield analogy.

How would we apply that to your personal life? how are you concentrating your forces in your personal life because you've only got so much time and so much energy and so much money and so much attention in your day, how are you concentrating those? Where are you putting all your eggs into? Which basket are you putting it into, the right basket or the wrong basket? Are you hitting problems where the enemy is strongest instead of where the enemy is weakest? Are you finding the weak spots? Are you finding the spots where your force can really have the most leverage? Most people don't even think about this stuff, they don't their energy and their focus is dispersed all over the place. They're doing 10, 20 different things in their career, in their relationship, and this and that, they are all over the place and what's happening is that nothing is really moving forward because they're not properly concentrating their force. See, everyone has limited resources, that's what makes it so important to concentrate those resources properly, not to waste them, not to piss them away.

In the fall of 2005, I find myself at the Military World Championship in shooting. I'm in the lead in the final, and I have one shot left to shoot. The target is 50 metres away, and the ten is 10.4 millimetres. What is it that determines if I shoot a nine or a ten? Is it the physics, the technique, the relaxation or the breathing?

No, those are abilities that everybody at that level has been training for years. It's all about the thoughts I think and why I think them.

This is what concentration is about. When I was 23 years old, I felt that I had a kind of capacity, an inner drive and an energy that I didn't really know how to handle. And it frustrated me, not knowing what to do or where to go in this world. I was completely lost.

And the only solution I could think of was trying to become best in the world at ... something. I had no idea in what. But I decided to become a world champion. I was quite athletic, but my helpful brother pointed out that I was too old to become a world-class sprinter. So I choose shooting. This determination brought me into the military arena, and since that very day, I started my practice.

Thousands of hours were spent on the shooting range.

I ate on the range.

I slept on the range.

And still today, I can remember that smell of lead and loneliness. I travelled all over the country, competing, for three years, but I lost over and over again, not getting any reward or recognition. In my world, I was programmed to win, but I didn't. And I couldn't understand how it could be so incredibly difficult. It was only my perseverance that kept me going. In this very moment at the World Championship aiming at the target with these irritatingly tight margins, and these nervous thoughts running through my head, this potential triumph could easily become yet another fiasco. But then, suddenly, I saw, and I focused on, a beautiful autumn leaf playing in the wind. I give this leaf my full attention. And suddenly, I am completely calm. And the world champion title is mine.

This action was a deliberate choice and the result of persistent mental training. Because this leaf relieved me of distracting thoughts and made me focused.

And the phenomena of concentration interested me more and more, not only in peak performance but also in the longer perspective and in life in general. I studied this vital capacity, and what I saw was that the human mind struggled with concentration on three distinctive ways.

First, our minds are often full of disturbing thoughts, often worried about not being good enough.

Second, instead of working with what we already know, we are constantly focused on what we will achieve.

And third, we are frustrated for not having time.

So, how can we help ourselves with these problems? Well, before we can discuss that, we need to find out what concentration is. In today's overflow, with new waves and trends, the ability to concentrate has been somewhat overlooked despite its great value. It's, however, a particularly complex function of our intelligent brain. So, let me simplify it for you. The pre-eminently thinking human beings, all of us in here, I guess, have the ability to think forward and backward in time. And we often go down the alarming path of thinking,

What happens if...?

What happens if I shoot a nine?

If I forget what to say having a presentation?

If I don't finish my report on time?

If I start losing followers on social media? If life doesn't turn out the way we had anticipated? Or we worry about why it didn't turn out the way we wanted it to.

Can we then, at moments of need, free ourselves from these disturbing and worrying thoughts, a kind of undemanding present arise? Because it's in this undemanding present that we are focused. It's here that we perform and function exactly as well as we are.

So, standing there, shaking with nervousness but giving that leaf my full attention, this is what happened.

So, concentration is simply about choosing the right thought among thousands of thoughts. Now, how do we get focused?

Well, firstly, regarding the disturbing thoughts. We need to learn to notice disturbing thoughts and to distinguish them from not disturbing thoughts. A not disturbing thought is something completely neutral, like a lamp, a chair, a belt, a toaster or an autumn leaf.

Because as the brain, in broad terms, only can concentration on one thing at a time, a not disturbing thought knocks out all the disturbing and worrying thoughts. And this is enough to reach that inner capacity we in fact already possess.

Second, regarding how we constantly concentration on what we will achieve. In the performance-based society of today, we often lose concentration because we constantly strive towards the new and better instead of finding our inner power and constructively working with what we are best at, at each given moment.

Because if we always think about the goal, about what we want to achieve, about where we want to go, about who we want to become, our concentration is constantly on the future and not on the work that needs to be done now. So, removing the goal now and then is not as crazy as it sounds.

Well, scary at first. I mean, where we're going now? But that is how concentration ends up on who we are and what we have instead of chasing after what we are not and do not have. So, concentration is not about becoming something new or something better, but simply about functioning exactly as well as we already are and understanding that this is enough for both general happiness and great achievements.

Third, regarding frustration for not having time. We live in a time with endless possibilities around us, and this seems to have created the notion that life must be lived intensely. We try to exceed on all arenas at the same time, and one's self-confidence ends up on all that we do instead of placing concentration on one thing and doing this really, really well.

Our concentration shatters into a thousand little must-dos and must-haves, and time is somehow eaten up. But the principle is quite simple: The more possibilities, the more there is to refrain from. Today is no longer about prioritizing but about prioritizing away. Imagine yourself sitting at your desk in the morning and making a must-to-do list.

Now challenge yourself and make a not-to-do list, and your brain will automatically shift in focus.

Also, it's funny, despite our unique ability to think long-term, we want immediate response on our efforts. Posting a picture on social media, for instance. We live our life with short-term focus, and we are losing the ability to build our own self-esteem without constant feedback from others. So, how do we find a long-term focus, that concentration that moves your life in the right direction? Achieving long-term concentration requires that we learn to direct our attention inwards.

To that what I call our inner core. To that which doesn't need a constant response. Because it's here, and perhaps only here, that we find genuine contentment and satisfaction with who we are.

So, why is all this so important to us all? Concentration is important because several essential abilities are linked to this innate skill. The ability to listen, to learn, to empathise, and not at least, to steer our self and our life in the right direction. And as the pace in our society will increase even more, it will require quite a lot to navigate in this new unpredictable era, with a constantly growing roar around us. And you know what? We must control the intense society.

The intense society must not control us. And for this, we need to stay sharp and focused. But do you know what I'm worried about? I am concerned that our ability to steer our concentration with our own power is something we are about to lose. I'm worried that we, in the future, will see two groups of people: those with the ability to co-exist and handle the intense society, and those who will become more or less slaves under the same possibilities. Although we as adults are struggling with our concentration more than ever, we still have a sense about what concentration is. But what about our coming generations? What if our generation is the last one with access to this life-affirming tool? Here, we own a responsibility in ensuring that this ability is maintained in the future. Because focus, this vital force, is what brings out the best in ourselves and in others, something our world so greatly deserves.

Now, finally, embrace the ability you have within yourself to be able to see the value of a small autumn leaf playing in the wind

PILLAR FIVE

Disciplined Execution and Tactical Follow Through

After you come up with a plan and you've gathered up your strategic resources, and you know where to concentrate your force. Now what you have to do is to execute the plan. A great plan poorly executed leads to disaster, great execution with a poor plan also really leads nowhere. It's highly inefficient, highly non-strategic. You need both a great plan and a masterly execution to achieve success. And most people are very poor executors. I have a book called how to get shit done. It talks about many important points about what it takes to get results.

To be a result maker in life, to really be good at execution this is something that you need to make a study of. At one point in my life, I just went all-out on execution, I just focused so much on execution because I knew that I need to get good at execution and I became a good executor. Now that's something that takes years, it takes years to really become a good executor, it's not something you can do in a week, especially if you spend the last ten or twenty years being a poor executor, you've developed all sorts of bad habits that now need to be unwired.

It's easy to have ideas. It's very hard to turn an idea into a successful product. There are a lot of steps in between it. It takes persistence, determination and relentless efforts. So, I always tell people who think they want to be successful or become entrepreneurs, you need a combination of stubborn relentlessness and flexibility.

And you have to know when to be which. And basically, you need to be stubborn on your vision. And because otherwise, it'll be too easy, to give up. But, you need to be very flexible on the details, because as you go along, pursuing your vision, you'll find that some of your preconceptions were wrong, and you're going to need to be able to change those things.

So, I think taking an idea successfully all the way to the market, and turning it into a real product that people care about, and that really improves people's lives, is a lot of hard work.

We've all got ideas. Everybody's got ideas. We can probably sit here for the next two hours, draw them all out, record them, and predict the next 78 great start-ups over the next ten years.

Uber was originally called Magic Cab, but the guys that execute it, sucked. So, they lost. So, if there's any level of romance, left about your idea, I'd like to suffocate it, because I think the actual situation is, what you actually do with it.

We all pay taxes, and we all hate the idea, that if you're losing that money. But, there's a difference, between hating that you lose that money, and hating to pay taxes. I love paying taxes. If it is the fair amount, and if it is used wisely, I think we all have to contribute to it, because that's how you set up social programs, that's how you build infrastructure, that's how you have a military, and all of those kinds of things. So, that's great.

But, I always has the belief that the money, that they're paying taxes, I want to make up, through wise investments. So, this is why I got into real estate, right away, in the 70s, and I started buying raw land, and developing that.

I started buying apartment buildings. And, you know, just think about it. I remember, in 1974, I bought my first apartment building, and we bought it for 215,000 dollars. It was then a lot of money. And I put only down, maybe 35, 37,000 dollars. But, within two years, the apartment building was worth, instead of the 215, 350,000 dollars, and I sold it. So, imagine now, how much gain there was, right? I mean, so we made hundreds of percent, of my initial investment. So, that's what I'm talking about. So, it takes thoughts, and ideas, can make much more money, than actual, physical labor. And physical labor is always part of the action, because I always say, you got to work your ass off, no matter what you do, because now, we have a great idea, but then, you still have to implement it, and you have to hustle. You have to go to the bank, get the financial statement, do this and that, and raise money sometimes, and you go, and look at the thousands of apartment buildings, to find the right one, and all of those kinds of things.

So, you still have to work. But normally, if it's just physical labor, you can never make the money that you can make when you have ideas, so this is why it's important.

I always tell people, I say, the secret is, is there are certain times, don't think. Like when you get up in the morning, don't think. Just roll out of bed, take a stroll or go to the gym, work out, you know that's what you have to do, and then, read something, and learn something. Don't even think about anything.

But, there are other times when you have to really think, and you really have to get creative, and have a clear vision of where you want to go, and what you want to do, and that's what I always had, and that's what I always believed in. I always believed in making money, so that then, you can do something with that. You invest in it, and all this, eventually, you create a family, and you get some of your kids in order, and stuff, but also, for charity

The reality is, reading a book, or going to a conference, or having a great conversation, where you get this golden information, that's all fantastic, but what makes mastery, is execution on the ideas, not the ideas.

And so, no idea works, unless you're willing to roll up your sleeves, do the practice, invest the time, put in the effort, and do the work. I think we've all observed a lot of people love reading the books. They love showing up at the courses. They do all the online training, and nothing ever changes. And they say, well, I don't know why it doesn't change, why my life doesn't change, why my thinking doesn't change, why my performance doesn't change, why my relationships didn't change. Well, it's because ideas don't work, if you don't execute on them. So, if you look at the great business builders, you look at any great performer, one thing that makes them great, is their grit. One thing that makes them great, is their hunger to practice. One thing that makes them great, is they're willing to sacrifice. I mean, yes, they're passionate, but do you know, the root of the word passion, is suffering?

You've got to be willing to suffer for your vision. You've got to be willing to suffer, to reach BIW, best in world. You've got to be willing to suffer the ridicule and laughter of your critics and your cynics, to get to a place, called world of class.

I think you know what you're supposed to do, deep down inside. I think everybody does, and a lot of people just don't go after it. And like most people start off, they say, I want to be this, but I'm going to get that, to make sure I have something to fall back on. And what you're doing is you're setting yourself up for failure because when you're going, there's a possibility that you will fall back. And when you put that out there, then you fall back. But, if you just say, hey, this is what I want to do, and you go do it, you usually get your stuff the way you want it. That's the way of the entrepreneur, he is actually going about, looking at the world, and finding problems. Some people think that's a negative mind-set, but actually, I find it as a curious mind-set. You're out there, looking for problems, looking for things, that aren't the way they should be, or could be.

Okay, you got a good idea. Look, everybody's got a good idea. Okay, everyone has an idea. Not everyone has a good idea, but lots of people have good ideas. Look, Uber's a good idea. You push a button, and get a ride. I don't know if you were the first person to think of that idea, but you are not the first person to do it. You got to just go do it, then. You got to just get out there, and go do it.

So, it's easy, to have the idea, or straightforward. But then, you've got to have enough guts, to go out there and try. And that's, that's the way of the entrepreneur. You need to execute, and you need to execute as fast as possible. Because, the thing at the end of the day is, whether you feel you have competitors, or not, sooner or later, you're going to have someone, and if you can't move fast enough, someone's going to beat you to the punch.

So, make sure whatever you're doing, you get something out, within a month or two. If it takes you longer than that, you're taking way too long. I created this company, called Serph, and it was in Rockwell, Texas, right by Dallas, and I had this brilliant idea. Have any of you guys heard of the Media Temple Grid Server solution? That was my idea, a year or two, before it came out. And I spent a million bucks on it, trying to actually do that idea, before Media Temple. The funny thing, is that I have a million bucks, so I had to actually borrow a million bucks, and I spent it on business partners, who moved really slow, and really wanted the best that they did.

Within 12 months, we launched nothing. They also had some of the problems, in my previous slide, right, like financial instability, and they had a family, and kids, I think like six.

So, I even bought them a home in Rockwell, Texas, that cost 200 and something thousand. Why did I buy it, instead of renting it? I have no clue, I was stupid and young. But nonetheless, I lost over a million bucks, on that, of borrowed money. Not investor money, but borrowed money, that I had to pay back. And it failed miserably, because we never launched anything.

If you can't launch something, someone like me, the tumble's going to beat you to the punch, get a ton of customers, and make a lot of money. So, lessons I learned from that, set deadlines, no matter what. You have to set deadlines. People have to be held accountable to them as well, right?

Can't just set a deadline, it passes, nothing happens, someone better be meeting them. If not, you know, something has to change. You also need to make sure they're small. At the deadline, if the milestones, goals, are too big for those deadlines, they're not going to get met. So, make them really small and tangible.

That way, you can see it, really well in advance, if they're actually going to be met, or not. And last, but not least, don't worry about perfection. A lot of people are like, dude, I'm going to create the most perfect version of, you know, whatever it may be.

That software has a lot of buzz. Mine's going to be perfect. Perfection is overrated. Nothing is ever perfect.

You're going to continue to have to iterate so forth, and so on. It's never going to be perfect. There's always going to be issues. Just get it out there, and start trying to make money. Strategy is five percent of the answer, and execution is 95 percent.

Yeah strategy is fine, it's very important. But, it's only five percent. If you don't go to execution after this, the delivery, and the performance of the company is going to be very weak. I really, I really believe it. Now, it doesn't mean that strategy's not important, but when you establish north, and you know exactly where north is, for the company, you've done something very important, because you're giving the direction. But, if you don't stop moving north, if you don't stop mapping, and establishing milestone, you're never going to be getting there.

People start what if-ing themselves, alright? They say, aw I got this great idea, but what if I do all this work, and it doesn't work? What if I put in all this time, and become an excellent employee, and I don't get promoted? What if, I put in all this work, to become an excellent salesman, and I don't sell?

What if, what if, what if? And I tell you, what if. What if, you don't do shit? Where are you going to be? Because it isn't going to be any better than where you are now. Alright? It's very easy for people who are in the beginning levels of success, or the beginning levels of their success journey, to tell themselves stories, that other people's circumstances are better than theirs, that the other people have rich parents, they've got luck, they've got better circumstances. They got less obstacles. And they say, and I understand, you know, that if you just do the work, you'll get the result.

But, what if? Okay, they want to believe it, they want to succeed, but at the end of the day, they don't do it, because they talk themselves out of it. Alright?

This is easily the number one thing that keeps people from succeeding. It's the number one thing that keeps people where they are. It's the number one thing that keeps people broke. It's the number one thing that keeps people in a situation of frustration or regret.

And what ends up happening is that they end up going through their life accepting what they're dealt, doing what they're told, and they end up at 50, 60 years old, wondering what the fuck happened.

Well, I'm going to tell you what happened. You talked yourself out of going after what you were supposed to go after. You talked yourself out of your purpose. You talked yourself out of the idea, that success is cause and effect, not magic luck, or magic fairy dust. That's what happened, okay?

And that's the number one thing that keeps people from succeeding. It's the what if story, that they tell themselves, over, and over, and over again, as to why they can't move forward, and other people can.

Why, if they do the work, it still isn't going to work out. Success is easy, guys! easy! It's making a plan, and executing the plan, every day. It's that easy. It's that easy. Okay, and people will always be like, Andy, it's not that easy! There's got to be luck to it! You know, f******, my friend, he created the super snuggy snowball machine, and it made 100 million dollars, in one day! Well, you ain't your f****** friend! You're a regular dude, just like me, and I'm telling' you, and you can choose to believe whatever the f*** you want to believe, but the reality is this. Make a plan, work the plan. Make a plan, work the plan. Make a plan, work the plan. And whenever the plan doesn't work, you change the plan! That's not called failure! It's called learning a lesson! It's called adjusting! On the run, you are not going to have a perfect plan, from start to finish, just because you thought of an idea. That's reality, okay?

So, when we talk about the what- if story, you're telling yourself, the- what-if story, you're trying to justify your fear with, it's bullshit. If you do the work, and you do it for a long enough time, and you have at least average intelligence, you will be successful. Period. End of story.

Now, you can accept that, or you can go out, and you can look for all the little exceptions. You can look for the, you know, the glory stories, the guys who make millions of dollars, in one year, which they don't. You know, it doesn't happen to the average guy. You go out there, and say, oh they got lucky, look. That's all luck, it's all luck. Or, you can accept the fact, that for people who don't get lucky, like us, that there is a way to still do it, which is to make a plan, and execute the plan, and do that relentlessly, consistently, over the course of ten years, and you'll be where you want to be.

I'm not a smart person, I'm not overly intelligent. I just make a list every day, and execute on it! I don't worry about what if. I don't think about, what if I do this, and it doesn't work out the way I want? I know that it'll work out in some way, and because I'm smart enough to adjust the plan, on the way, I know that it will at least end up somewhere close to where I want to be. It's not that hard.

Quit over-complicating it. There are no what ifs. If you do the work, the result will be there, period. - Well, the last, and the most valuable lesson, as an entrepreneur, I learned, was about the value of execution. Way too many people. Way too many people, spend too much time, thinking about the vision.

We are taught, that you have to build a better mouse trap. Every venture capitalist will tell you that to be a successful entrepreneur, you need a breakthrough innovation. Well, you have to assume, none of us, or at least most of us, are not the smartest people in the world. There are lots and lots of great, great inventors out there.

How are we going to be the person, who's going to always build a better mouse trap?

Well, to be successful, you don't have to build a better mouse trap. You just have to build a different mouse trap. And as long as you're executing well, the business, all of this, comes down to block and tackle. It's not about the great vision, it's always about the great execution.

And you can always succeed, by out-executing your competitors, not necessarily having the best product in the marketplace. And I think that Microsoft is a great example, where they took a same product, that other people may have had, but they executed substantially better, and today, the market leader in the industry.

PILLAR SIX

Adaptability Strategy

I'm going to move on to the next pillar which is adaptability. Strategy is not about selecting the ultimate one best strategy and then going with it forever, that's actually a mockery of strategy. Proper strategy is all about being flexible and adaptable, it's about understanding that the environment is constantly changing every day. What the battlefield looks like today and tomorrow might be totally different. It might rain tomorrow, that will totally change the battlefield, the troops might lose their morale tomorrow, this totally changes the situation that we're dealing with, they might be out of food tomorrow or out of water or half of them might be dead, and it totally changes the situation.

So whatever plans I have tonight, by tomorrow morning, I'll have to be able to adapt in case things change, and I have to plan in such a way that I don't have this rigid plan that tells me, when X happens, then Y happens, then Z happens and they'll all just go swimmingly according to plan. No, you have to plan for all the contingencies, and you have to plan for all the disasters, all the misfortunes that might happen.

See, a common naive mistake that people make when they do personal developments is that they just think well, okay, let me just come up with a three-year plan for my life, and then what happens? A month later, all of a sudden you're not following that plan at all because your plan is over here and then real life is over there and they're just a golf apart. No, that doesn't work! High quality strategy requires that your plan be flexible. Take into account all sorts of different scenarios and contingencies, and you have to be able to sit down and rewrite the plan every week and every day if necessary.

Be flexible, don't get too rigid, don't get dogmatic about your plan, don't get attached and cling to your plan as though it's your baby, and it's the only thing. If this is the only way it's got to be is through this plan, no, that's very poor strategy. You'll get slaughtered if you do that, you've got to be adaptable. A lot of times, people start a new business, they come up with a business plan and they think that this is how it's going to go, this is how my business going to generate money, and then in reality it doesn't work. That is a naive business plan, this is the person who starts business for the first time and of course, they fail pathetically. They fail miserably because to get a successful business model going, you have to try a lot of different stuff. You have to experiment, you have to see what actually works in the marketplace, what actually works on the battlefield. A lot of times, this stuff is unknown, you're dealing with a lot of unknown variables you're not going to have all the Intel, you're never going to have perfect Intel which means that you have to be very adaptable you have to be willing to change your business plan completely, throw it out and get a new business plan.

Some of the most successful businesses started out with one idea of how they're going to earn money and that didn't work and they went in a totally different direction and then they made billions. PayPal is an example this.

PayPal as a business started out as a mobile payment processing for Palm Pilots and that of course didn't work, and then they got the bad idea hey, why don't we just email each other payments, let's create a system that allows people to email each other money and then they came up with PayPal, generating billions of dollars. But see they were flexible enough to change because if they just stuck with their original idea they would have gotten nowhere, they would have went bankrupt. That's very important that's why I always talk about open-mindedness, and how important open-mindedness is.

Most people are so stuck on dogma and their beliefs about how life is, and how spirituality is and religion has to be this way, and education has to be this way. Personally, I can't afford to be rigid, because to be the most strategic I can be, I have to be extremely adaptable. I have to be willing to throw away everything I believe. And in a sense everything I believed and do believe will get eventually replaced and thrown away because there's always better beliefs, there's always better models, there's always better something better to come and replace whatever you currently hold true.

I have interviewed a lot of people who say that they hate change. During my stint in the staffing business and human resources arena, I got the opportunity to spend a good amount of time with thousands of people; interviewing, hiring and placing them to work with companies like Google, Sony Computer Entertainment, Bank of America and other. And when I hear those words, "I hate change" I immediately would get fearful for them because frankly, the one thing you can count on in this life is change, impermanence. In fact, if you think about change, it's a great opportunity. If it wasn't for change, new opportunities wouldn't exist, everything would be static. So, embrace change, make it your friend, hug it and navigate your life based upon opportunity, not fear. And a lot of people I talked to weren't doing that, no! When someone said to me, 'you know I'd hate change' it would make me think that they weren't ready to navigate into new worlds, they weren't ready to adapt, they weren't ready to change, they weren't ready to make that first great, or next great step forward either in their careers or private life.

Life is a machine that's constantly evolving, and if you're not ready for the next turn, you will miss your opportunity. The engine could blow at the beginning of your career, at the middle or towards the end, you just got to get in the game. What does that really mean? In my days as a human resource personnel, I met a lot of young people that just weren't ready to get in the game. In fact, they were looking to self-actualize maybe at the age of 22 or 23. Well, the reality is that we know that's not going to happen, and they would sit around and wait for the perfect role, the perfect job, and they wouldn't even be prepared for it. They wouldn't be starting to think about alignment until their senior year in university or college.

So to me this whole concept of change, of staying in the game, doing repetitive work in the game not just viewing it from outside is absolutely critical, and then once you're in the game there's this concept of maybe you don't have to make huge change but you got to pivot a little bit. Well, you got to adapt and I think you know if you're driving down the highway, and all of a sudden you see traffic coming at you, well, you change lanes or you get the heck out of the way, or if you're driving down the highway and you want to get there a little more quickly, you navigate, you change lanes maybe you take an exit.

You have a vision, you have an objective, you have a goal, as you are trying to attain that goal, you may see the market shift, you may see circumstances change, and you may see new opportunities that exist right before your very eyes. If that's the case, adapt, modify, change direction, pivot so to speak and go into that slightly new direction. That's what pivoting is all about.

Well if you pivot and fail, congratulations. You can know you start by failing forward. If you take a deep reflection of your life. The greatest lessons that we ever learn come from our moments of failure. When I look back on my life personally, it's not the wins, or the successes, or the great deals that I closed, or that we closed as a team back in business. It's what I didn't get, the deal that I lost, when I missed a free throw in a game that I learnt from the most. Because when you fail, you take a clinical approach towards your life, and you say how can I do better next time? What was it that I missed, or I should have done? What can I do to plan and prepare so the next time I have a greater chance at victory, a greater chance of success, a greater chance at that promotion.

The greatest thing about failing if you're going to move forward is the next opportunity to make another decision. I mean life is about a series of decisions, and you're going to take actions or not take actions. If you don't take actions, you're not taking risks, you're not learning new things. If you're not taking risks you're typically probably not going to fail, if you don't fail it's hard to move forward. I stated it earlier that failure is a recipe for success. Yeah, it's a recipe for lifelong learning. Show me a person who has never failed they've probably never been highly successful because they haven't taken risk

The person that has the most behavioural flexibility is the person that is in control of any situation. Not the boss, not you know, nor the person that has the most power or the person that uses the most force. It's the person that is most flexible, the person that can take on any situation, go with the flow and be flexible.

PILLAR SEVEN
Study of Principles

The last principle or the last pillar of becoming a highly strategic thinker is the study of principles. Regardless of how chaotic a situation may be, there are principles that can give shape to your thinking about the situation and help you emerge victorious. You need to study the proper principles of battles if you're a general preparing for war, you need to study the principles of business if you are an entrepreneur, and you need to study the proper principles of life and self-actualization if you're a human being trying to live your ordinary life.

It is the study of the principles that make life amazing it's all the principles that control your psychology and how life works and how relationships work and how interaction with people works, how your mind works.

Some of these principles have been known for thousands of years, but most people don't make a study of it and you might say, well, I'm already reading this book. Well, that's good but you're just reading this book but there's a big difference between reading this book and making a study of these principles. Someone who makes a study of self-actualization principles is like someone who sits down read books and watches videos from start to finish take notes on everything, re-reads his notes, study his notes in the morning, and then at night again and then washes the video again, drills it into his subconscious mind and then he thinks that he contemplates it deeply.

He doesn't just accept what I say. He thinks about it, he integrates it into his own world view, he combines multiple sources, cross-references everything, and checks everything against his own intuition make sure everything is fitting in.

Someone who engages in real study of principles is someone who is not just looking for a fix, he's looking for a deep understanding and a mastery of the principles of life. That's a whole other level of commitment and dedication and of course, it yields to a whole other level of results, which is why I want to convince you and sort of psych you up to get excited about learning these principles.

I want you to make this a lifelong process, I want you to get excited about self-actualization as I am in my own life.

Conclusion

So these are the seven principles and seven pillars rather I should say of strategic thinking. This is what it takes. Your life will only become satisfying once you start to make wise strategic decisions that's the only way it's going to happen.

You know in the movie Pulp Fiction, I like that movie. Towards the end, there's a scene there with Samuel L. Jackson and he was getting robbed and he has to give his wallet up to the thieves and then later he asked for the wallet back and they give him the wallet back and on the wall and it says bad motherfucker in big letters bad motherfucker on it's kind of embroidered on the wallet I really like that, and I was thinking about that scene today and I thought you know what would be even better if it said strategic motherfucker on that wallet strategic motherfucker because that's how I think about myself in my own life, and how I want you to think about your life from now on is that you are going to be a strategic motherfucker using these principles and pillars that I talk to you about.

Your whole attitude towards life needs to change from the complacent lazy one you've been having to this one where you're a strategic motherfucker, where every move you make, every step you take has a purpose in mind where you're almost Machiavellian about every action that you take, not a neurotic negative way. I'm not mean, I'm not saying that you should go and cheat people, rip them off, I'm not saying that you need to be all manipulative like that. I'm just saying you've got to be very clear about every single step you're taking, where it's leading you, why you're doing it, what the priority is and then how it fits into the bigger picture of everything for you, and then what kind of resources you need to develop in order to allow you to do that.

I've been a strategic motherfucker since I was seven years old. It just probably came naturally to me. I don't know why other people aren't this way but since seven years old I've been thinking about what my career is going to be, and exactly how I'm going to do it and where I'm going to go to school, what am I going to learn, what degrees am I going to get. I'm always thinking like 20 years ahead how much money am I going to have, what that money's going to allow me to do, where am I going to live, what if I do this, what about that?

My mind just doesn't stop with this, it just keeps going. Just the other day I was thinking about what the end of my life is going to look like. What do I don't want to look like when I'm 70 years old on my deathbed. What do I want to achieve. What do I want my legacy to be? You can apply strategy to anything you want. A loving relationship apply strategy to that. If you want to raise great kids, apply strategy to that. This isn't just related to work or to earning money, in fact you know earning money and just going to work and running a business, it's actually kind of natural to be strategic, most people tend to be strategic there, where they're not strategic is in their personal lives and their spiritual lives in their love lives in their whole attitude towards life.

I'm extremely strategic in what I ultimately want out of my life. My ultimate strategic intent in life is to die knowing that I lived well knowing that my life not that it mattered in some global sense to people that's kind of silly I don't really care about that these days, what matters to me is that I can look back over my life before I die and I can say yeah that that was the way I wanted to live my life, that was it. I don't have any regrets I didn't piss my life away. I had this one life I knew from an early age I knew that this was the only one I'm going to have and then I'm going to make something of it that I'm proud of. And that's what I worked for and that's what I got that's my ultimate strategic intent.